Concept: Michael Williams
Written by: Michael Williams & Djehuti-Ankh-Kheru
Researched by: Michael Williams & Djehuti-Ankh-Kheru
Layout and Design: Cindy Soso

Picture Credits:
Dr. Mae Jemison – Melody M. McDowell c/o The Jemison Group,
Dr. Rose-Marie Toussaint, Dr. Elizabeth Rasekoala,
Dr. Dale Emeagwali c/o Donita Brown, Ursula Burns c/o
Christa Carone, Dr. Patrica Bath, Sophie Redman c/o
African Surinamese Organisation, Dr. Kathleen Okikiolu,
Shirley Ann Jackson c/o Theresa Bourgeois

Published by: BIS Publications

First published 2007
First reprinted 2010
Reprinted 2015

BIS Publications:
Tel:+44(0)7903 791 469
SKYPE ID: bispub
web: www.bispublications.com
email: info@bispublications.com

ISBN: 9781903289983

Dutch Translation: Zwarte Vrouwen als Wetenschappers & Uitvinders
ISBN: 9789079576036

A catalogue record for this book exists in the British Library.

© 2007 Copyright Michael Williams
© 2007 Copyright Djehuti-Ankh-Kheru

All rights reserved. No part of this publication may be reproduced,
stored in, or introduced into a retrieval system or transmitted in any form or
by any means; electronic, mechanical, photocopying, recording or otherwise,
without prior permission from the copyright holders of this book.

Disclaimer:
Whilst every effort has been made to provide accurate information, neither the authors or the publishers shall
have any liability to any person or entity with respect to any errors, omissions or inaccuracies contained herein.

In Memory of Janet Narh

WHATEVER THE
MIND CAN CONCEIVE
AND BELIEVE
YOU CAN ACHIEVE

YES
YOU!

Dedicated to:
The Girls Who Are Motivated To Reach For The Stars As They Become Women

ACKNOWLEDGEMENTS

Michael Williams

I would like to thank both my friends and foes as both have challenged me to be the best I can be. Also the valiant women I have met on my journey. All those who continue to support BIS Publications titles and finally to the one who makes this all possible the Creator.

Djehuti-Ankh-Kheru

I would like to thank Mrs. Yvonne Beeldsnijder for supporting me and all the projects I get involved with unconditionally, Mr. Emmanuel Ashikodi Osakwe for his advice, and last but not least everybody I forgot and feels he or she needs to be thanked.

Introduction

Most mainstream books on scientists rarely mention any black or women scientists. The few women scientists whose careers are discussed are never women of colour. Although there are some works that do portray black scientists, most of those more liberal endeavours tend to overlook the contributions of black women and likewise keep up the myth that scientific talent is restricted to gender.

Even the authors of this book are not totally free from guilt in this respect, when discussing the often overlooked contributions of black scientists and inventors in general we have been asked the question more than once both by men and women *if there actually are black women scientists and inventors?*, We must admit that is a fair question. Although we have portrayed black women scientists before, we hope to address the above question with this work more specifically.

We found it important to portray women from different areas and social backgrounds. We have portrayed several women who are achievers in science and engineering. However, we have also paid attention to some extent to those who were not perceived to be scientists, but still came as close to becoming so as the limits of history had allowed. Taking into account the limits placed upon them, they earn our utmost respect. We hope you will enjoy reading this book as much as we have enjoyed presenting it to you.

Structure of Book

This title is presented as 12 biographies, split over two sections, each with six biographies written and researched by each author.

Each biography is concluded with the author's summary. After each biography there are questions and an extra question section to engage the reader.

The answers to the questions can be found in the back of the book along with a time-line, a glossary and bibliography section for extra reading.

Black Women Scientists & Inventors Volume One

Contents Page

I	Acknowledgements
I	Introduction
I	Structure of Book
II	Contents Page

Section 1: Michael Williams

1	Dr. Rosemarie Toussaint
3	Dr. Mae Jemison
5	Dr. Dale Emeagwali
7	Madam C.J. Walker
9	Dr. Elizabeth Rasekoala
11	Mary Seacole

Section 2: Djehuti-Ankh-Kheru

13	Dr. Sophie Redmond
15	Ursula Burns
17	Hypatia
19	Dr. Shirley Ann Jackson
21	Dr. Kathleen Adebola Okikiolu
23	Dr. Patricia Erna Bath

	Answers
25	Section 1
26	Section 2
27	Glossary
29	Time Line
30	Bibliography
32	Catalogue

Dr. RoseMarie Toussaint (1957-)

Never Question the Miracle

Haitian-born, Dr. Rose-Marie Toussaint is the first female of African descent to become a director of a liver transplant service. Dr. Toussaint is a strong believer in obstacles as supreme teachers and incubators for emotional, spiritual and professional growth.

There is no doubt that these beliefs are the reason for her success in a field largely dominated by European males. Documenting her extraordinary journey in *Never Question the Miracle - A Surgeon's Story*, Dr. Toussaint hopes to inspire parents and educators to provide extra-curricular activities to encourage children to be ambitious and realise their dreams.

Dr. Toussaint mentors children with a message that success comes through hard work, and when one reaches the top of his or her field, it can be as exciting as it is rewarding. She attributes her success in the remarkable survival rate of her transplant patients to God first and her skills second.

A Fellow of the American College of Surgeons and the International Transplantation Society, Dr. Toussaint believes that we should refer to ancient and traditional preventative methods of healing.

These methods include improving our diet by eating lots of fruit and vegetables, regular exercise, and taking moments to be silent in order to communicate with our inner voice.

Dr. Rose-MarieToussaint has trained in Holistic and Ayurvedic medicine and is a Yoga and Qi Qong teacher. She manages her own Massage Therapy (RMT) Holistic Complementary and Integrative Medicine practice and is the founder and chairperson of the National Transplant Federation in the USA, an organisation whose main aim is to increase knowledge of how to avoid transplants.

Dr. Rose Marie Toussaint - Questions

1. Which country is Dr. Toussaint from? Haitian
2. Name two organisations of which Dr. Toussaint is a member? AFOtA COS)(ITS) ✓
3. Dr. Toussaint is the first woman of what service? Africa descent ✗
   liver transplant serise
4. What medicine has Dr. Toussaint trained in? liver transplant servise/ Hotichns and ayurvide ✗
5. Which organisation is Dr. Toussaint the founder? National transplant and redication 0
6. What does Dr. Toussaint say about success? remarkable survial ✗

2/6

EXTRA QUESTIONS

1. What is Yoga and where did it originate?
2. What course of study would you need to take to become a qualified medical doctor?
3. Can you name the surname of another famous Toussaint from Haiti and what makes the other Toussaint famous?
4. What is a Stethoscope, what is it used for and draw one?

Author's Summary
Dr. Rose-Marie Toussaint shows us that regardless of race or gender, an individual must believe in his or her abilities, work hard, learn from failures, and see obstacles not as negatives, but as advantages which can help develop one's convictions.

Dr. Mae Jemison (1956-)

Sky's Not The Limit

Mae Jemison is an African-American who was born on October 17th, 1956 in Decatur, Alabama, USA. She was raised in Chicago where she spent most of her childhood and teenage years.

At the age of 16, she attended Stanford University on a scholarship and graduated with a Bachelor of Science (BS) degree in chemical engineering and fulfilled the requirements for a Bachelor of Arts (BA) degree in African/African American studies. It was here that she developed an interest in biomedical engineering.

She then attended Cornell University Medical College where she earned her doctorate in medicine (M.D). Prior to joining the National Aeronautics and Space Administration (NASA) in 1987, Dr. Jemison worked in both engineering and medicine.

Dr. Jemison spent two and a half years as the Area Peace Corps medical officer for Sierra Leone and Liberia in West Africa (1983 - 1985) and was a Peace Corps volunteer in Cambodia. On her return, she worked as a General Practitioner (GP) in Los Angeles, USA, while updating her engineering skills.

At the age of 31, Dr. Jemison had the honour of being selected from over 2000 applicants to participate in an astronaut training program at NASA, USA. On September 12th, 1992, she became the first woman of colour to go into space aboard the space shuttle Endeavour. She spent a total of 190 hours, 30 minutes and 23 seconds in space. She resigned from NASA in March, 1993.

Dr. Jemison's current work focuses on the beneficial integration of science and technology into daily life. She founded the Jemison Group Inc., a small company that assesses the worldwide social and technological circumstances of users of new technology. Dr. Jemison also established a number of projects including The Earth We Share™ (TEWS), an international science camp for young people designed to build critical thinking and problem solving skills through an experiential curriculum. As director of the Jemison Institute for Advancing Technology in Developing Countries and professor of Environmental Studies at Dartmouth College in the USA, Dr. Jemison works on sustainable development. This means she assesses methods that improve the quality of human life now, such that future generations can grow and prosper.

Dr. Jemison is a noted lecturer and has received many honours and awards, including the Essence Science and Technology Award and the Kilby Science Award. She was inducted into the National Woman's Hall of Fame and the National Medical Association Hall of Fame and has received numerous honorary doctorates. Outside of these professional achievements, Dr. Mae Jemison's hobbies include dancing and reading and she currently lives in Houston, Texas with her cat Little Mama.

Black Women Scientists & Inventors Volume One

Dr. Mae Jemison - Questions

1. When and where was Dr. Jemison born?
   [handwritten: October 17 1956, Alabama Decatur USA]

2. How many degrees does Dr. Jemison hold and name them? *[handwritten: 2 BS and BA]*

3. Which parts of the world has Dr. Jemison's medical work taken her? *[handwritten: African America]*

4. Name the projects Dr. Jemison currently works on and what are the aims of these projects? *[handwritten: NASA]*

5. What honours and awards have Dr. Jemison received?

6. Was Dr. Jemison the first woman of colour in space? If yes, what was the name of the shuttle and when did it take off?

7. Does Dr. Jemison still work for NASA?

8. What does the phrase 'sustainable development' mean?

EXTRA QUESTIONS

1. Dr. Jemison spent a total of 190 hours, 30 minutes and 23 seconds in space. Work out the total number of: seconds, minutes, hours, whole days, whole weeks, whole months.

2. What is space? (Find out about the solar system).

3. What is an astronaut?

4. What is meant by the word experiential?

Author's Summary
Dr. Mae Jemison shows us that nothing is too far to reach; not even the sky's the limit.

Dr. Dale Emeagwali (1954 -)

My husband is a genius but sisters are also doing for themselves...

Dale Emeagwali was born Dale Brown on December 24th, 1954 in Baltimore, Maryland, USA to Leon and Johnnie Brown.

She was the youngest of three children. Dr. Emeagwali attended Alexander Hamilton Elementary School in Baltimore. In 1972, at the age of seventeen, she graduated from North-Western Senior High School.

As a young girl, she always liked science and did well in mathematics.

Her parents taught her and her two brothers fun facts about science by demonstrating simple experiments. Her father liked mathematics and he had a small collection of math books, which he used to show his children tricks using numbers.

In 1976, Dr. Emeagwali attended Coppin State College in Baltimore, Maryland, where she earned a Bachelor's of Art Degree in Biology, with a minor in Chemistry. She then attended Georgetown University School of Medicine in Washington, D.C., and in 1981 she achieved a PhD in microbiology.

Dr. Emeagwali has been a multi-disciplinary research scientist for over twenty years in government laboratories and universities. Her areas of expertise include microbiology, cell biology, biochemistry and molecular biology. She was the recipient of the "1996 Scientist of the Year Award of the National Technical Association".

Dr. Emeagwali has worked extensively in cancer research and molecular biology. She was one of the first to show that the cancer gene, oncogene ras, could be inhibited or weakened by a technique known as anti-sense methodology. In the field of biochemistry, she developed a system for analysing an important cellular protein.

In the area of virology, her work with a DNA virus demonstrated how genes can be manipulated to make organisms use limited genetic material more efficiently.

In the field of bacteriology, she discovered the existence of two forms of enzyme in a soil micro-organism and the streptomyces bacteria. Prior to this finding, the enzymes were known only to exist in higher organisms. This discovery is important in the area of evolution because it has helped lead the way in the search for other proteins in bacteria that were previously thought to be unique to higher organisms.

Dr. Dale Emeagwali is currently on the faculty of Morgan State University in Baltimore, Maryland. She is married to the eminent computer scientist and mathematician Dr. Philip Emeagwali, they have a son called Ijeoma.

Dr. Dale Emeagwali - Questions

- 1. When and where was Dr. Emeagwali born?

- 2. As a child what school did Dr. Emeagwali attend?

- 3. What subject did Dr. Emeagwali like when she was a child?

- 4. Dr. Emeagwali and her two brothers were shown what by her father?

- 5. After leaving high school how many years did it take Dr. Emeagwali to complete her studies?

- 6. What are Dr. Emeagwali's areas of expertise?

- 7. In 1996 what award did Dr. Emeagwali receive?

- 8. Dr. Emeagwali has worked extensively in which fields?

- 9. What are the names of Dr. Emeagwali's son and husband?

EXTRA QUESTIONS

- 1. What does the abbreviation MBA mean?

- 2. Biology is the study of .... (please complete).

- 3. Find out the names of 5 proteins.

- 4. What role do enzymes play in digestion?

Author's Summary

Dr. Dale Emeagwali's work is extremely important in the understanding of all living things which includes humans. Through her work, one day cures for illness such as cancer will be found. Although Dale Emeagwali is a mother and wife, she shows us that she can also be an eminent scientists.

Madam C.J. Walker (1867 - 1919)

At One Time the Richest Woman in America

Madam C. J. Walker was born Sarah Breedlove on December 23RD, 1867, in Delta, Louisiana, USA.

Her parents were ex-enslaved Africans who had become sharecroppers on their ex-master's farm. She was the youngest of three children. At the age of seven, her parents died from yellow fever.

This was a time in America's history where the country was very much segregated into black and white.

There were very little prospects for employment or education for black people unless they set up those institutions for themselves.

Her brother left home to find work, and after they lost the farm, Madam C. J. Walker and her sister went to work as laundry assistants. She married at the age of fourteen to Moses Macmillan with whom she had a child.

In 1887, at the age of twenty, her husband was killed in an accident. Madam C. J. Walker then moved to St. Louis where she married John Davis and worked for a black-owned hair-care company called Poro Co. After this unsuccessful marriage, Walker moved to Denver to live with her brother's family where she was employed as a cook. After noticing that her hair had begun to fall out, she began experimenting with products of her own to remedy her situation.

One night she dreamt of a black man who told her where to go to locate the right ingredients for a hair growing solution. Madam C. J. Walker, with the help of family and friends, produced Wonderful Hair Grower™, Vegetable Shampoo™ and Glossine™ after months of rigorous trials. She later invented a hot-comb. This is a metal comb which is heated over a stove burner.

Madam C. J. Walker became a door-to-door sales agent for her products. This financed her newspaper advertisements, which brought in mail orders for her products. In 1906, she married Charles Joseph Walker, who was a salesman for a black-owned newspaper; she later adopted his name. They expanded the product lines and employed staff who shared in the profits from the sales as the demand for the products grew rapidly. Madam C. J. Walker opened schools and colleges in cities across America and the Caribbean to train women with her hair-care products.

Although Madam C. J. Walker could not read until later on in her life, she became the first African-American woman millionaire in America. She was also a caring and compassionate woman. She donated $10,000 to young black men and women to further their education and sponsored six students to attend the black-run Tuskegee Institute.

Black Women Scientists & Inventors Volume One

Madam C.J. Walker - Questions

- 1. What year did Madam C. J. Walker's parents die and what did they die of?

- 2. What is a sharecropper?

- 3. What products did Madam C. J. Walker invent?

- 4. How did Madam C. J. Walker come to invent her solutions?

- 5. How did Madam C. J. Walker help other people?

EXTRA QUESTIONS

- 1. How did Madam C. J. Walker let people know about her inventions?

- 2. What are advertisements?

- 3. What is an entrepreneur?

- 4. How was Madam C. J. Walker an entrepreneur?

Author's Summary

Although Madam C.J. Walker received very little academic education and was born during the harsh cruel times of the enslavement of African people, she had a belief in herself and a knowledge that the Creator knew she was much more than what some people said she was. Madam C.J. Walker went on to invent several products and to become the richest woman in America at that time.

Dr. Elizabeth Rasekoala (1960 -)

Helping others realise their true potential

Elizabeth Rasekoala was born on 17th May 1960, in Lagos, Nigeria. As a child, Dr. Rasekoala was interested in Maths and Chemistry.

In 1983, she attended Ahmadu Bello University where she obtained a Bachelors Degree in Chemical Engineering. Dr. Rasekoala continued her education by travelling to the UK, where she gained a Masters Degree in Chemical Engineering in 1986 at the University of Manchester.

Dr. Rasekoala has now worked in the chemical engineering industry for over twenty years in both Nigeria and the UK. focusing much of her energy on education

Being involved in the education of African Caribbean students, particularly in the areas of maths, science and technology, Dr. Rasekoala found that many black students in the UK were under achieving in these subjects; subsequently, she decided to start the UK based African Caribbean Network for Science and Technology. She also initiated the Ishango Science Club and RESPECT campaign.

Dr. Rasekoala has written about the achievements of black students in science in local and national press as well as in academic journals. She has been a keynote speaker in the USA, Canada, South Africa and in many European countries. She is a member of Business in the Community: Opportunity 2000 - National Focus on Women panel; Qualifications and Curriculum Authority (QCA) - Advisory Group on Race; and many other professional societies in the Chemical Engineering field.

In January 1991, Dr. Elizabeth Rasekoala received a commendation from the Commonwealth Association of Science, Technology and Mathematics Educators (C.A.S.T.M.E) for innovation in recognition of her work in conceptualising and developing the Ishango Science Club in the UK.

The African Caribbean Network for Science is a national educational charity, set up in 1995 by black professionals working in various fields of science, engineering & technology. The purpose of the organisation is to advance the educational achievements and career aspirations of black youth in these areas where they are very much under - represented, due to inequalities of the mainstream educational system within the U.K.

Extra Notes: The Ishango bone dates back to 20,0000 BC.
It was found in a small African Village bordering Zaire and Uganda.
It's the oldest instrument found to date which man used for counting.

Black Women Scientists & Inventors Volume One

Dr. Elizabeth Rasekoala - Questions

- 1. Which universities did Dr. Rasekoala attend?
- 2. What subject did Dr. Rasekoala study, and what degrees has she obtained?
- 3. Why did Dr. Rasekoala found the African-Caribbean Network for Science?
- 4. When does the Ishango bone date back to and where was it found?
- 5. To study chemical engineering at university which subjects do you think you need to be good at whilst at school?
- 6. What did Dr. Rasekoala receive in January 1991?

EXTRA QUESTIONS

- 1. How did the Ishango bone get its name?
- 2. What is the study of bones called? (clue: Look in Black Scientists & Inventors Book 3)
- 3. Explain what is meant by a network of:
    a) people,?
    b) computers?
    c) shop?
- 4. What is the total population of Nigeria?
- 5. Nigeria has some of the finest oil the world has to offer, can you name 1 or 2 petrol companies which extract Nigeria's oil for sale around the world?
- 6. Name two countries in Africa where pyramids more than 1000 years old can be found?

Author's Summary

Although Dr. Elizabeth Rasekoala has become very successful in her area of science, she has shown a selfless attitude towards others. She wants others to also benefit from the rewards of a successful career in science. Her extra curricular activities are helping hundreds and thousands of children in the UK realise their dreams.

Mary Seacole (1805 - 1881)

The "Mother Seacole"

One of the greatest contributions Jamaica has given to the world is the "Yellow Doctress" otherwise known as Mary Seacole.

Mary Seacole was born in 1805, in Kingston, Jamaica. Her father was a Scottish army officer and her mother was a Jamaican of African decent who kept a boarding house principally for army officers.

Growing up in the military, Seacole became fascinated with several aspects of army life such as travel and exploration.

When Seacole was twelve she was sent to England; when she returned to Jamaica she became even more excited about travelling and had developed an interest in nursing.

In 1852, a Cholera outbreak swept across the Island of Jamaica. Seacole was of great service as she treated many of the sick with her own herbal medicine remedies that she had learnt from her mother. Around the same time, she travelled to Panama where Cholera was also raging and she became invaluable there too. In 1853, she returned to Jamaica where Yellow Fever was now raging; again, she was of great service nursing the sick back to health by administering her remedies.

In 1854, England, France and the Ottoman Empire (Turkey being at the centre) fought against Russia; this was known as the Crimean War. Seacole travelled to England offering her nursing services; however, she was refused because of her race and gender. Nevertheless, she continued to offer her services to the War Office and Florence Nightingale's own organisations, but each time she was met with an adamant "NO". Seacole still determined, she made her own way to the Crimea. Once in their she volunteered her services to various military hospitals and nursed the wounded and dying soldiers on the battlefield. The Officers and men loved her and referred to her as "Mother Seacole" soon enough, she was managing her own institution, which she called The British Hotel. The British Hotel served as a combination of a store, a dispensary, and a hospital for British officers.

Mary Seacole died in 1881 in England. She is buried in St Mary's Catholic Cemetery in Kensal Rise, West London.

Sir William Howard Russell wrote of her *"..I trust that England will not forget the one who nursed her sick and who sought out her wounded to aid and succour them and who performed the last office for some of her illustrious dead."*

Black Women Scientists & Inventors Volume One

Mary Seacole - Questions

- 1. Where and when was Mary Seacole born?

- 2. When did the Crimean War begin?

- 3. Which countries were involved in the Crimean war?

- 4. What is the name of the fever, which raged in Jamaica?

- 5. What was the name of the hotel, which Mary Seacole ran?

- 6. On what basis was Mary Seacole refused when she offered her nursing services to both the British War Office and Florence Nightingale?

- 7. What did the officers and men that loved her refer Mary Seacole as?

EXTRA QUESTIONS

- 1. In which sea can the island of Jamaica be found?

- 2. What continent did the majority of Jamaicans come from?

- 3. To date Jamaica has one female national hero can you name her and why she is considered a hero?

- 4. Turkey (the country) was once a part of which empire?

Author's Summary
I think Sir William summed Mary Seacole up best and I can't really add to that.

Black Women Scientists & Inventors Volume One

Dr. Sophie Redmond (1907-1955)

Doctor, may I ask you something?

As a youth Dr. Sophie Redmond had many disagreements with her conservative father, one of these disagreements concerned her choice of profession.

As a youth Dr. Sophie Redmond had many disagreements with her conservative father, one of the disagreements concerned her choice of profession.

Her father, who was a teacher, strongly disagreed with her and tried to dissuade her from trying to become a doctor. He thought that to be a teacher was the highest level a black woman could achieve; and believed his daughter would not receive a fair chance to get her Medical diploma.

Nevertheless, Dr. Redmond persisted and became the first black woman doctor in Suriname, despite the many belittling remarks she had to suffer during her studies because she was both a woman and black.

After Dr. Redmond had finished Medical School, she settled in Paramaribo, the capital city of Suriname (which is situated in South America and was a Dutch colony at the time) as a family doctor. Dr. Redmond sympathized with the lower social classes and women in general, and did what she could to support them. She treated poor patients for free on numerous occasions. Dr. Redmond became known as the datra fu potisma (doctor of the poor).

The common people of Suriname began to call their beloved female doctor 'dokteres' (doctress), Dr. Redmond ran a popular radio programme called Datra, mi wan aksi yu wan sani (doctor, may I ask you something?). On the radio programme, health problems were discussed in such a way that anybody could understand it; they were presented in a dialogue in Sranang Tongo, which is the linqua franca of Suriname (a language that was not appreciated by the authorities and middle class blacks), where doctor Dr. Redmond played a people's woman role.

The doctress became also known as a playwright and an actress, these plays served their purpose; as they were another means to raise the cultural awareness of the black masses. As a woman who promoted Sranang Tongo and African Surinamese culture in general, she often wore traditional African Surinamese dress. Dr. Sophie Redmond also participated in her countries politics, but at that time the Surinamese political system was arranged in such a way that an independent woman politician did not stand a chance to be elected.

Dr. Sophie Redmond - Questions

1. Where did Dr. Redmond live?

2. Where is Dr. Redmond country situated?

3. Why didn't Dr. Redmond's father want her to go to Medical School?

4. Why was Dr. Redmond's radio programme so appealing to the common people?

5. What name did Dr. Redmond's patients prefer to call her?

6. Dr. Redmond was a doctor, but could you name another activity Dr. Redmond was known for?

EXTRA QUESTIONS

1. Can you name an important inventor who was born in Suriname? (Clue: Look in Black Scientists & Inventors Book 1)

2. What did that person invent?

3. What is the name given to the freedom fighters who fought against the colonial establishment in countries like Suriname and Jamaica?

4. Those freedom fighters are known for the strong resistance they put up, but can you name something else they are known for?

Author's Summary

Many people who eventually become successful in their lives had at least been encouraged by their own family to be the best that they can be. Unfortunately this was not the case with Dr. Sophie Redmond. Nevertheless she succeeded against the odds and became a role model for black women in her country.

Black Women Scientists & Inventors Volume One

Ursula Burns (1958-)

Heading a Major Company

Ursula Burns is the current president of Xerox Corporation. She grew up in poverty in a single parent home in New York.

Mrs. Burns went to a Catholic high school, where she fell into trouble with the teachers because she had organised a union for black students, and was punished for being involved with its activities.

As Burns was an excellent student she received a scholarship to attend the Polytechnic Institute of New York, where she earned a B.A. in science.

As an intern Burns had already worked for the Xerox Corporation, but after graduation she was employed by this company which was recruiting African American students at the time. With the financial support of this company, Burns was able to go to university and earn herself a master's degree in engineering.

Burns did very well at Xerox, by becoming an executive assistant and was promoted in rank numerous times. She has also led several business teams. Burns really proved her value to the company when she improved a copier.

In 1997, Xerox had developed a new digital copier which copied, printed, scanned and faxed; a development that had taken six years and billions of dollars. Unfortunately, the machine didn't work the way it was expected to, but Burns came to the rescue. She analysed the problems and presented her solutions to the executives.

She changed last-minutes design flaws and reduced the time it took to manufacture the machine from nine hours to three. This multi-functional digital copier became Xerox Corporation's best-selling product.

Ursula Burns was promoted to the top of the company, head of Worldwide Manufacturing, later becoming it's Senior Vice President for Corporate Services. Besides this she still holds several appointments and as we have learnt she eventually became the President of Xerox Corporation in 2007.

Ursula Burns - Questions

- 1. In what type of family did Mrs. Burns grow up?

- 2. Why did Mrs. Burns get in trouble with her high school teachers?

- 3. In which company did Mrs. Burns become president?

- 4. In what capacity did Mrs. Burns start working for that company?

- 5. Name one product which Xerox sells?

- 6. What was Mrs. Burns' contribution to the top selling product of the company?

EXTRA QUESTIONS

- 1. Can you name two other black women who have headed / head large companies?

- 2. Can you name an important black leader who resided in New York?

- 3. Can you name another black inventor who has made a contribution to printing?

- 4. Can you tell which people were excluded from major unions in the U.S. for a long period of time?

Author's Summary
Mrs. Ursula Burns career is very remarkable, growing up in a poor single parent home, becoming an outstanding engineer, due to excellent performance quickly rose to the top of a major company and eventually became its president. It can be said that *nothing succeeds like success!*

Hypatia (± 370-412)

From the Mists of Antiquity

Hypatia who was born in ancient Egypt was one of the most brilliant female scientists in human history. The civilization of Egypt had flourished for thousands of years, but Hypatia lived in a time when it was no longer in the hands of the native African population.

It was now dominated by foreign powers. In those days Egypt was evidently no longer the powerful country it once had been.

Hypatia was from the city of Alexandria, a city that was not only famous for its tall lighthouse, but also for its library (which was the largest in the world at the time), as well as its many learned citizens.

Although Egyptian, Hypatia spoke and wrote in Greek, because Greek was the international language in those days. This is similar to how Jamaican scientists speak and write in English todays, but that doesn't make them less Jamaican.

As a daughter of the Egyptian mathematician Theon, she was allowed to walk around freely without a male accompanying her. This clarifies that Hypatia was not Greek, because Greek women were not allowed to walk around freely in those days, unlike their Egyptian counterparts. Also note that ancient Egyptian women arguably enjoyed more rights than many women in the world today; for example equal pay for equal work.

Hypatia was a Professor in the University of Alexandria and she lectured on mathematics, philosophy, physics and astronomy. She also invented an apparatus for distilling water and measuring the level of liquids. Unfortunately, Hypatia was brutally murdered on the streets by a group of fanatic people in the year 412.

Even before Hypatia was born, there had been black women scientists in countries like Egypt, but still the life of Hypatia shows that there have been black women scientists for a very long time.

Black Women Scientists & Inventors Volume One

Hypatia - Questions

- 1. In which city did Hypatia live?
- 2. What was the city Hypatia lived in famous for?
- 3. In what language did Hypatia write and lecture?
- 4. What could Egyptian women do that Greek women were not allowed to do?
- 5. What had Hypatia invented?
- 6. Can you name one subject which Hypatia lectured on in the university?

EXTRA QUESTIONS

- 1. Can you name another ancient civilization from the African continent?
- 2. Can you name two other famous women from the civilization of ancient Egypt?
- 3. Can you name another famous African scientist from antiquity?
- 4. Do you know the name of the Greek philosopher who studied in Egypt for 22 years, he is also well known for 'his' mathematical theorem?

Author's Summary
Hypatia's life teaches us that there have always been outstanding black women, and that black women on the African continent in antiquity, in some respect were more emancipated than many present-day women.

Dr. Shirley Ann Jackson (1946-)

Aim for the Stars so that you can Reach the Treetops

Shirley Ann Jackson is a theoretical physicist who has held senior leadership positions in government, industry, research, and academia in the United States of America.

She is the President of the oldest technological university in the United States, Rensselaer Polytechnic Institute.

She is the former chairman of the U.S. Nuclear Regulatory Commission (NRC), a Federal commission which has the responsibility to oversee power plants that provide approximately 20 percent of the electricity produced in the United States.

Born in Washington D.C., Dr. Jackson grew up in a family which stimulated her to get the best out of herself. Her mother read her biographies of famous black people. Her father always told her *"to aim for the stars so that you can reach the treetops"*.

As a child Dr. Jackson collected and stored bees for fun, and observed them closely. When she started to approach her hobby scientifically she won first place prize at a science fair. Dr. Jackson attended Massachusetts Institute of Technology (MIT), considered to be one of the best research universities in the world. She would eventually become the first black woman to earn a PhD. from that university. Whilst at MIT, Dr. Jackson led a successful effort to increase the number of black students attending the university.

Dr. Jackson believes that more black people should become scientists as scientists can advise government leaders on policies that relate to science and technology, which inevitably affects as all.

Dr. Jackson has held numerous important jobs and positions. She worked as a scientific researcher for AT&T Bell Laboratories; she taught physics to college students; and she has served on the board of directors of several major corporations, including a bank, an electric power company, and a company that makes medical devices. In 1995 U.S. President William J. Clinton appointed her to be the chairman of the NRC. The NRC is charged with the protection of public health and safety in the civilian use of nuclear materials.

Therefore, as Chairman of the NRC, Dr. Jackson had the ultimate authority for public safety in the event of a civilian nuclear emergency. Since 1999, Dr. Shirley-Ann Jackson has been the President of Rensselaer Polytechnic Institute, in Troy, New York.

Dr. Shirley Ann Jackson - Questions

- 1. Where did Dr. Jackson grow up?

- 2. What did Dr. Jackson's mother do to stimulate her interest in learning?

- 3. What reason did Dr. Jackson give in terms of black people getting involved in science.

- 4. What does NRC stand for?

- 5. What are some of the tasks of the NRC?

- 6. Which university did Dr. Jackson become President of in 1999?

EXTRA QUESTIONS

- 1. Can you name a well known black university which is located in Washington D.C.?

- 2. Can you name the man who redesigned the city of Washington D.C. from memory when everything seemed lost?

- 3. Can you name another famous black physicist?

- 4. Can you name a famous university for black women in Atlanta?

Author's Summary

Even though Dr. Jackson was one of the very few black women at one of the best polytechnic universities in the world, she did not let herself be discouraged, and eventually became one of the foremost scientists in the U.S., which proves black women can definitely reach the top of their professions.

Dr. Kathleen Adebola Okikiolu (1965-)

Mathematics Flowing Through her Veins

Kathleen Adebola Okikiolu is a great mathematician in her own right, she is the daughter of a notable Nigerian mathematician and inventor George Okikiolu, who has written nearly 300 scientific papers, more than any other black mathematician. As the daughter of this Nigerian mathematician and a British mother who teaches mathematics, one might argue that mathematics flows through her veins.

Dr. Okikiolu studied at Cambridge University, and continued her studies in the U.S. where she received a PhD in mathematics in 1991. Dr. Okikiolu was appointed in various positions at several renowned universities as an instructor, visiting assistant Professor, and an associate Professor.

Dr. Okikiolu is the recipient of several awards; she was the first black person regardless of gender to win the prestigious Sloan Research Fellowship in 1997. This is an award for the most promising young mathematics researcher. The same year Dr. Okikiolu received yet another award for outstanding young mathematicians, scientists and engineers, the PECA award.

Dr. Okikiolu was one of the sixty young researchers who were awarded the Presidential Early Career Award for Scientists. This award was established by President Clinton in 1996 in order to cultivate and reward the finest scientists and engineers around the world.

Dr. Kathleen Adebola Okikiolu is socially very active, for instance she has coordinated workshops and created mathematics curricula for inner-city children. Also her Presidential Early Career Award for Scientists and Engineers (PECASE) video project is worthy of mention, the video features inner-city children teaching and learning mathematics.

Black Women Scientists & Inventors Volume One

Dr. Kathleen Adebola Okikiolu Questions

- 1. What subject had Dr. Okikiolu's father and mother studied?
- 2. Can you name something special which Dr. Okikiolu's father has achieved?
- 3. What is the name of the prize the U.S. Government gives to the sixty most outstanding young scientists, mathematicians and engineers?
- 4. Why was the particular prize established by former President Bill Clinton?
- 5. Can you name another award of which Dr. Okikiolu was the recipient?
- 6. Can you name a social project Dr. Okikiolu is involved in?

EXTRA QUESTIONS

- 1. Can you name two people who reside in Nigeria?
- 2. What art form were the people of Southern Nigeria famous for?
- 3. Can you name two other modern-day Nigerian scientists?
- 4. Can you name another famous black mathematician?

Author's Summary
Dr. Kathleen Okikiolu had the advantage of both parents being mathematicians, but still that doesn't take anything away from her own admirable achievements in mathematics, and the social projects she is involved with.

Dr. Patricia Erna Bath (1942-)

As if He was Interviewing Einstein...

Patricia Bath is an ophthalmologist, this is a doctor who studies and treats the diseases of the eye. As a teenager, Dr. Bath already had made a name for herself as a scientific researcher in a different field of medicine, having been involved with cancer research programs. She got the chance to do this because she was such a promising high school student.

Dr. Bath was allowed to visit Yeshiva University and Harlem Hospital to do her research. It was here Dr. Bath collected and analysed information, developed a hypothesis and created a mathematical equation to predict cancer cell growth.

At the International Scientific Congress Dr. Bath was highlighted as one of the co-authors that contributed to the important research in the prediction of cancer cell growth.

At the time journalist Harold Preece interviewed teenager Dr. Bath, he was very impressed by her answers that he said afterwards that he felt like he had interviewed Einstein; a scientist of the highest calibre.

Preece considered Dr. Bath as one of the two most intelligent women he had ever interviewed in his career as a reporter. As a seventeen year old, Dr. Bath was recognized as one of the most talented young scientists in the U.S.A. After having finished college she trained in ophthalmology and became an assistant surgeon. Despite the cancer research she had conducted as a teenager she would eventually become a distinguished internationally known ophthalmologist and surgeon.

Dr. Bath became more and more interested in the treatment of eye diseases with the aid of laser technology in particular cataracts. Cataracts is a condition affecting the eye, where the lens becomes dark, causing partial or total blindness. It is not unusual for people to get cataracts when they get older. She consulted with several experts in the field which took her as far as Berlin University in Germany.

With the help of the information she acquired in Germany, Dr. Bath invented a laser instrument which removes cataracts; the Laserphaco Probe. This invention, patented in the USA in May 1988 revolutionised eye surgery. Dr. Patricia Bath has improved upon her apparatus several times since and has four patents to her credit.

Dr. Patricia Erna Bath - Questions

- 1. What is an opthalmologist?

- 2. What kind of research did Dr. Bath conduct when she was a teenager?

- 3. What did an experienced journalist say about Dr. Bath?

- 4. What are cataracts?

- 5. Which people are more likely to get cataracts?

- 6. What has Dr. Bath invented?

EXTRA QUESTIONS

- 1. Can you name a medieval West African city which was famous for its doctors who could cure cataracts?

- 2. Can you name a black pioneer in laser technology?

- 3. Can you name another famous black surgeon?

- 4. Can you name another black woman doctor who has done cancer research?

Author's Summary

Dr. Patricia Bath' scientific talent blossomed when she was just a teenager. Dr. Patricia Bath would eventually become a world renowned ophthalmologist and invent the Laserphaco. This invention is to the benefit of all mankind, which makes Dr. Patricia Bath one of our best examples that black women inventors not only do exist, but have made great contributions to science.

Black Women Scientists & Inventors Volume One

Answers to Section 1

Dr. Rosemarie Toussaint

1. Haiti
2. Dr. Toussaint is a fellow of the American College of Surgeons and a member of the International Transplantation Society
3. The Liver Transplant Service
4. Holistic and Ayurvedic medicine
5. National Transplant and Federation
6. Success comes through the application of hard work

Dr. Mae Jemison

1. October 17th 1956 in Decatur, Alabama, USA.
2. (3), BSc in Chemical Engineering, BA in African and African American studies, Doctorate degree in Medicine.
3. Sierra Leone and Liberia in West Africa and Cambodia.
4. The Earth We Share promotes critical thinking and problem-solving skills. The Jemison Group Inc. concentrates on making science and technology work in everyday life. The Jemison Institute for Advancing Technology in Developing Countries promotes sustainable development.
5. Dr. Jemison is in the National Women's Hall of Fame, the National Medical Association Hall of Fame and has been awarded many honorary doctorates. She was also awarded The Essence Science and Technology Award, the Kilby Science Award.
6. Yes. Endeavour, 1992.
7. No, she left in March 1993.
8. 'Sustainable development' means to apply methods that improve the quality of human life such that future generations can grow and prosper.

Dr. Dale Emeagwali

1. December 24th 1954 Baltimore, Maryland, USA.
2. Alexander Hamilton Elementary School, Baltimore.
3. Science.
4. Simple experiments at home.
5. 1981-1976 = 5 years.
6. Microbiology, cell biology, biochemistry, molecular biology.
7. Scientist of the Year.
8. Cancer research and molecular biology.
9. Ijeoma and Philip.

Madam C.J. Walker

1. 1874. Yellow fever is a viral disease carried by mosquitoes. The symptoms of yellow fever begin to appear 9 - 12 days after receiving a bite from a mosquito carrier. The virus damages the liver and causes a yellowish bile pigment to gather in the skin. Other symptoms of the disease are fever, headaches, dizziness and muscle ache.
2. A person most likely an ex-enslaved person who owns a share of a landlord's land.
3. Hair grower solutions, hot-comb.
4. She lost her hair, experimented with various products and saw the ingredients in a dream.
5. She sponsored disadvantaged children to finish their education. She employed lots of black women in her factories and schools.

Dr. Elizabeth Rasekoala

1. Ahmadu Bello University and Manchester University
2. Chemical Engineering, Masters & Bachelors
3. She noticed that many black students in the UK were under achieving in the subjects of math and science.
4. The Ishango bone dates back to 20,0000 BC. It was found in a small African Village bordering Zaire and Uganda.
5. Science, Physics, Chemistry and Math.
6. A commendation from the Commonwealth Association of Science, Technology and Mathematics Educators (C.A.S.T.M.E).

Mary Seacole

1. Kingston Jamaica, 1805
2. 1854
3. England, France and Turkey fought against Russia
4. Yellow
5. The British Hotel
6. Her Gender and Race
7. Mother Seacole

Black Women Scientists & Inventors Volume One

Answers to Section 2

Dr. Sophie Redmond

1. Suriname
2. South America
3. He thought his daughter would not get a fair chance to ever get her diploma because she was both a woman and black
4. Because health problems were discussed in such a way that everybody could understand it: they were presented in the lingua franco of Suriname
5. The dokteres (the doctress)
6. She was also known as a playwright and an actress

Mrs Ursula Burns

1. In a single parent family
2. Because she had organised a union for black students
3. Xerox Corporation
4. As an intern
5. copiers, scans, fax machines, etc.
6. She had analysed earlier mistakes that had been made, changed design flaws and cut the time to manufacture the machine from nine hours to three hours

Hypatia

1. Alexandria
2. Its tall lighthouse, its library and its many learned citizens
3. She wrote and lectured in Greek
4. Unlike Greek women Egyptian women were allowed to walk around freely
5. An apparatus for distilling water and measuring the level of liquids
6. She lectured mathematics, philosophy, physics and astronomy

Dr. Shirley Ann Jackson

1. She grew up in Washington D.C.
2. She read her biographies of famous black people
3. Because a number of scientists can advise governments on their policies, so if black people are not involved with science it will not be to the betterment of their political power
4. Nuclear Regulatory Commission
5. To oversee power plants, the protection of public health and safety
6. Rensselaer Polytechnic Institute

Dr. Kathleen Adebola Okikiolu

1. Mathematics
2. He has written nearly 300 scientific papers: that is more than any other black mathematician
3. The PECA Award
4. To breed and reward the finest scientists, mathematicians and engineers around the world
5. The Sloan Research Fellowship
6. The PECASE video project

Dr. Patricia Erna Bath

1. A doctor who studies and treats the diseases of the eye
2. She conducted cancer research
3. He felt like he was interviewing Einstein
4. Cataracts are a condition affecting the eye, where the lens becomes dark, causing partial or total blindness
5. Aged people
6. The Laserphaco; a laser instrument which removes cataracts

Glossary

A
Apparatus - The tools or other pieces of equipment that are needed for a particular activity or task.
Appointment - A job or position of responsibility.
Astronaut - Some one who goes into space in a spacecraft.
Atom - The smallest part of a chemical element that can take part in a chemical reaction.

B
Bacteria - Tiny creatures which we can not see with just our eyes, There are good and bad bacteria. Bad bacteria can cause disease.
Biography - The story of a person's life written by somebody else.

C
Cell - The smallest unit of living matter that can live on its own. All plants and animals are made up of cells.
Cholera - A serious disease which affects the stomach and bowels.
Cancer - A disease in which the cells in someone body grows in way that's not healthy
Complementary - Given free to someone
Complementary Medicine - Medical treatment that is not part of the usual scientific treatment in Western countries, for example acupuncture.

D
Dispensary - A place where medicines are made and given out.
DNA - The chemicals in the cells of animals and plants that carries genetic information and is a type of nucleic acid.

E
Executive - A person who has an important job as a manager of a company or an organisation
Engineer - A person whose job involves designing and building engines, machines, roads, bridges, etc.
Empire - A group of countries which is controlled by one ruler.
Entrepreneur - Someone who starts a company .
Enzyme - Chemicals in living things such as plants and humans which causes chemical changes in other substances.

G
General Practitioner (GP) - A doctor who does not specialise in any field of medicine and has a surgery.

H
Haitian - A person who was born in the country Haiti.
Holistic - To focus on or deal with the whole rather than individual parts.
Hypothesis - An idea or explanation that is based on a few known facts but that has not yet to be proved to be true or correct.

Glossary

I
Intern - An advanced student whose training is nearly finished and who is working in a particular place to get further practical experience.

N
Nuclear energy - A powerful form of energy produced by converting matter into energy splitting the nuclei (= central parts) of atoms

O
Observe - To see or notice
Organisation - A group which a lot of people belong to. They may get together to do something.
Organise - To plan something to happen the way you would like it to happen.

P
Plant - A factory or place where power is produced or an industrial process is taking place.
Polytechnic - A college for higher education, especially in scientific and technical subjects

R
Revolutionize - To completely change the way that something is done.

S
Scientific paper - An academic article about a particular subject that is written by and for specialists.
Scholarship - An amount of money given to somebody by an organisation to help pay for their education.
Sharecropper - A farmer who gives part of his or her crop as rent to the owner of the land.
Streptomyces - Remedy which is characterized by its capacity to kill bacteria
Surgeon - A medical doctor who is trained to do surgery (=medical operations that involve cutting open a person's body).

T
Transplantation - A medical operation where for examples an organ from someone's body is taken and placed in another persons body.

U
Union - An association or a club for people with the same interest.

V
Virus - A very small living thing which cause disease and illness.
Virus (Computer) - A computer programme which causes your computer to function incorrectly.

TIMELINE

412	Hypatia is brutally murdered by a mob of fanatics
1805	Mary Seacole is born in Kingston, Jamaica
1854	The Crimea war starts.
1867	Madame C. J. Walker is born in Delta, Louisiana, USA
1881	Mary Seacole dies and is buried in West London, England
1907	Dr. Sophie Redmond is born in Paramaribo, Suriname
1919	Madame C. J. Walker dies leaving millions of dollars
1942	Dr. Patricia Erna Bath is born in New York City, USA
1946	Dr. Shirley Ann Jackson is born in Washington DC, USA
1954	Dr. Dale Emeagwali is born in Baltimore Maryland, USA
1956	Dr. Mae Jemison is born in Decatur Alabama, USA
1956	Dr. Rose-Marie Toussaint is born in Haiti
1958	Mrs Ursula Burns is born in New York City, USA
1960	Dr. Elizabeth Rasekoala is born in Lagos, Nigeria
1965	Dr. Kathleen Adebola Okikiolu is born in London, Great Britain
1988	Dr. Patricia Erna Bath patents the Laserphaco probe
1991	Dr. Elizabeth Rasekoala receives the C.A.S.T.M.E commendation
1992	Dr. Mae Jemison becomes the first woman of colour to go into space
1995	Dr. Shirley Ann Jackson becomes chairman of the NRC
1996	Dr. Dale Emeagwali receives the 'Scientists of the Year Award'
1997	Dr. Kathleen Adebola Okikiolu receives PECA award
1999	Dr. Shirley Ann Jackson becomes president of Rensselaer Polytechnic Institute
2007	Mrs Ursula Burns becomes president of Xerox Corporation

BIBLIOGRAPHY

Black Scientists and Inventors Book 1,
A. Henry and M. Williams, BIS Publications, 1999, ISBN: 9781903289006

Black Scientists and Inventors Book 2,
A. Henry and M. Williams, BIS Publications, 2003, ISBN: 9781903289020

Black Scientists and Inventors Book 3,
M. Williams, BIS Publications, 2007, ISBN: 97819032890

Heroes of the Caribbean
A Henry, BIS Publications, 2003

Black Africa - The Economic and Cultural Basis for a Federated State,
C.A. Diop, Lawrence Hill & Co. 1978, ISBN: 0-88208-096-2

Black Apollo of Science - The Life of Ernest Just,
K.R. Manning, Oxford University Press, New York, ISBN: 0-19-503299-3

Black Inventors from Africa to America,
C.R. Gibbs, Three Dimensional Publishing, 1995, ISBN: 1-877835-87-0

Black Scientists of America,
R.X. Donovan, National Book Company, 1990, ISBN: 0-89420-265-0

Blacks in Science - Ancient and Modern,
edited by Ivan Van Sertima, Journal of African Civilisation Ltd, Inc, 1983, ISBN: 0-87855-941-8

Collins Gem English Learners Dictionary 1980, ISBN: 0-00-458336-1

Geddes & Grosset Dictionary of Science, 992, ISBN: 1-85534-099-2

Our Story, edited by Akyaaba - Sebo and Ansel Wong,
LSPU/LBH 1988, ISBN: 1-8700 13 11-1

African American Achievers in Science, Medicine, and Technology,
Wina Marche, 1st Books Library, ISBN: 1410728943

African Americans in Science, Maths, And Inventions,
Ray Spangenburg & Kit Moser, Facts On File, John Wiley & Sons ISBN: 0816048061

African American Women Scientists & Inventors,
Otha Richard Sullivan & Jim Haskens ISBN: 047138707-X

Blacks in Science - Ancient and Modern,
Ivan Van Sertima editor, Transaction, 1992 ISBN: 0878559418

Black Women in Antiquity,
Ivan Van Sertima editor, Transaction, 1992 ISBN: 0878559825

Black Women in Scientists in the United States,
Winni Warren, Indiana University Press, 1999 ISBN: 0253336031

The Legacy of Black Scientists & Inventors vol 1,
Djehuti-Ankh-Kheru, 2003, ISBN: 9080672645

The Legacy of Black Scientists & Inventors volume 2,
Djehuti-Ankh-Kheru, 2006, ISBN: 9080672688

Zwarte Diamanten & Parels,
Djehuti-Ankh-Kheru, 2002, ISBN: 9080672629

Oxford Advanced Learners's Dictionary,
2005 ISBN: 13: 978-0-19-4316064

Other titles available from Michael Williams
Black Scientists & Inventors Book 1
Black Scientists & Inventors Book 2
Black Scientists & Inventors Book 3
Zwarte Vrouwen als Wetenschappers & Uitvinders Vol 1 - Dutch Version
Mr & Mrs Ken and the numbers 1 to 10
Simply The Best

Other titles available from Djehuti-Ankh-Kheru
The Legacy of Black Scientists & Inventors Volume 1 and 2
The Legacy of Black Scientists & Inventors Volume 1 and 2
Zwarte Vrouwen als Wetenschappers & Uitvinders Vol 1 - Dutch Version
The Other Side of the Story: The Golden Ages of Africa.

Notes

Catalogue
Other Must Have Books

Black Women Scientists & Inventors Vol 1
Black Scientists & Inventors Book 1
Black Scientists & Inventors Book 2
Black Scientists & Inventors Book 3
Valiant Women: Profile of African Women in Struggle

Coming Soon !

Black Scientists & Inventors Work Book
Blacks in Mathematics Work Book
Scientists & Inventors of Our World

Notes from the publisher
For more information on our titles please call us on:

Tel: + 44 (0) 845 226 4066
Skype: bispub
E: info@bispublications.com
W: www.bispublications.com

Using the contact details above you can request or download our catalogue. **All our authors are available to give presentations and workshops at your school, library, or book group.**

If you or your child enjoys our publications why not become a reseller? **Give us a call today.**

If you don't see our books in your child's school, library or bookshop please give them our telephone number. We can get it to them within a couple days